THE
ONE-MINUTE
BIBLE
GUIDE

TERRY GLASPEY

HARVEST HOUSE PUBLISHERS

EUGENE, OREGON

Cover by Franke Design and Illustration, Minneapolis, Minnesota

Thanks to Peggy Wright, Steve Miller, and Carrie Sue Halupa for their invaluable help and insight.

THE ONE-MINUTE BIBLE GUIDE
Copyright © 2008 by Terry Glaspey
Published by Harvest House Publishers
Eugene, Oregon 97402
www.harvesthousepublishers.com
ISBN-13: 978-0-7369-2323-1
ISBN-10: 0-7369-2323-3

Printed in the United States of America

08   09   10   11   12   13   14   15   / BP-NI /   8   7   6   5   4   3   2   1

Contents

BEFORE WE GET STARTED...

The Bible. It's the book that everyone quotes from, most people say they respect as the Word of God, and few people actually read. It's the source of much of our law, our art, and, of course, our faith. It isn't always an easy book to read and understand, but it *is* a book worth reading.

Sure, it's long. And much of it seems foreign to us. Some of it is kind of confusing. Some of it is hard to understand. Some of it frankly seems a little weird to the modern reader. The events recorded in it took place a long time ago, and it was originally written in languages that few speak or write today. But it is a book worth reading.

Countless people through many generations have found it to be a life-giving book, filled with hope, help, and strength for dark times. I know that I have! In its pages we glimpse the majestic glory and tender heart of its main character—God. And in its pages we are offered the promise of salvation through Jesus Christ, His Son. So, yes, it is a book worth reading.

But maybe you need a little help getting started. Well, the book you hold in your hand is intended as a guide to help you get more out of the Bible by 1) understanding how it all fits together, 2) discovering how you can get more out of reading and studying it, and 3) exploring how it can change your perspective on life's struggles. All these features are put together in sections that can be read in one minute or less. Think of it as a compact tourist guidebook for seeking out the treasures of the most amazing volume ever penned, or as *CliffsNotes* for the Scriptures.

I've tried to keep it simple, straightforward, and practical. My prayer is that you'll find within these pages the background you need to have to read the Bible with greater understanding. I also pray that it will deepen your appreciation for the miracle that is God's Word. Hopefully it will be fun too. So join me for this journey through the world's greatest book, one definitely worth reading.

Terry Glaspey

SEVEN WAYS THE BIBLE HELPS US KNOW AND LOVE GOD

1. *The Scriptures give us spiritual insight.*
   (Psalm 119:30; James 1:2)

2. *The Scriptures give us guidance.*
   (Psalm 119:105)

3. *The Scriptures produce faith in us.*
   (Romans 10:17)

4. *The Scriptures help us face temptation.*
   (Psalm 119:11)

5. *The Scriptures teach us wisdom and equip us for life.* (2 Timothy 3:14-17)

6. *The Scriptures are a mirror to our soul.*
   (Hebrews 4:12)

7. *The Scriptures nourish us.* (1 Peter 2:1-2)

Part One

~~~

Reading the Bible
for Yourself

FIVE REASONS YOU SHOULD READ THE BIBLE

1. *It contains a unique message from God—no other book can claim to be the "Word of God."* It is an inspired (2 Timothy 3:16-17) account of God dealing with His people and the written record of the life and teachings of Jesus Christ, who was Himself the eternal Word of God (John 1:1). If it's God's book, isn't it worth your time to explore?

2. *It is filled with practical wisdom about how human beings should live their lives.* In its pages you'll find advice on how to build a stronger relationship with God and with others, as well as the ethical rules necessary for living a more healthy and successful life. It shows us the best way to live.

3. *It teaches us the truth about God, about ourselves, and about the world we live in.* The Bible is a wonderful mirror in which to see our own limitations as human beings and

learn to depend on God. It is a book that transforms lives!

4. *It is the single greatest fountainhead of Western thought and culture.* You can't really understand the history of philosophy, law and politics, the meaning of much of our great art and literature, or even the significance of countless common English expressions without some knowledge of the Bible.

5. *It makes for a fascinating read!* Really! Whoever told you that the Bible was boring and irrelevant evidently hadn't read very much of it…or maybe they just read those tedious bits in Leviticus and the genealogies. The Bible is full of amazing stories, challenging teachings, and intriguing ideas. Give it a chance, and you'll see what I mean!

FIVE WAYS TO APPROACH READING THE BIBLE

1. **Reading at Random.** This is how many people read the Bible. They simply pick up their Bible, let it fall open to a random page, and then start reading. The problem with this is you'll often miss the all-important context of the passage and overlook many of the wonderful nuggets that you'd find with a more systematic approach.

2. **Reading Chapter-by-Chapter.** Many people (myself included) have discovered the joy of making a commitment to reading a chapter of the Bible every day. It adds inspiration to your life and helps you explore the entire Bible.

3. **Reading Book-by-Book.** We need to remember that the Bible was not originally written with chapters and verses. These were only added later to help us find specific sections and passages. Instead, each book

was its own scroll. There is a lot to be said for setting aside a significant block of time and reading a whole book of the Bible at one sitting. It's the way we'd read any other book, so why not read the Bible this way?

4. **Reading by Themes.** Another interesting way to explore the Bible is to trace various themes throughout the whole Bible, discovering everything it has to say about any given topic. You can use your concordance or a topical Bible to help in your exploration.

5. **Reading with Prayer.** There is an ancient Christian practice called *Lectio Divina*, which teaches the art of meditating on a verse or short passage and praying it into your life. Phrase-by-phrase you can praise God for the truth you see written on the page, examine your own life in view of what you are reading, and ask God to make it real to you.

EIGHT STUDY TOOLS EVERY BIBLE READER SHOULD OWN

1. **A Study Bible**. It can be of great assistance to have some explanatory notes, book introductions, maps, and charts right there between the covers of your Bible. There are a number of good ones available, but my personal favorite is *The NIV Study Bible,* or if you want something simpler, *The Student Bible.*

2. **A Notebook**. It's always a good idea to have a notebook handy to write down the insights you discover, passages you find helpful, or questions you'd like to explore later.

3. **A Concordance**. A concordance lists all the places any word is used in the Bible. It is helpful for examining what Scripture teaches about a particular topic and for finding a passage you remember when you can't recall where it is found. You probably have one in

the back of your Bible, but may want to get a more extensive one like *Strong's Concordance*.

4. **A Bible Dictionary**. The Bible dictionary provides brief definitions of words you might run across in your Bible reading, as well as brief biographies of key people in the Bible stories.

5. **A Topical Bible**. This handy tool groups together all the Scripture verses on any topic you might want to study. Be aware that these groupings are based upon the interpretations of the person who put the book together so take time to explore the context before you change any of your views based on what you read.

6. **Manners and Customs of the Bible**. There are several good resource books that help you understand the often-puzzling customs of Bible times. Check them out.

7. **A Bible Commentary**. A commentary helps the reader interpret Bible passages. Of course

scholars are merely putting forward their own views, so it is a good idea to compare how several commentators might provide different interpretations of the same passage. Commentaries can cover the whole Bible in one volume or be so detailed that one volume focuses solely on a single book of the Bible.

8. **A Bible Atlas**. This type of atlas is very helpful to see exactly where an event took place and the relationship between two localities. The atlas found in a good study Bible may be adequate for most readers.

TWELVE WAYS TO GET MORE OUT OF READING THE BIBLE

1. *Pay attention to the context.* Every verse is surrounded by other verses, so it is essential that you read in the context of the entire passage, the chapter, and the book. It isn't wise to just rip a verse out of context and try to apply it to your life.

2. *Focus on the main points and don't get tripped up on secondary issues.* Some people have arrived at very strange conclusions about what the Bible teaches because they have focused on some obscure and unclear passage and dreamed up their own interpretation.

3. *The most obvious interpretation is probably the correct one.* Don't make a Scripture passage more complicated than it actually is or look for encoded messages or hidden mystical teachings. Most of the Bible is relatively straightforward, but...

4. *Don't take metaphors literally.* When Jesus

said, "I am the Door," you shouldn't be
looking for a doorknob. Allow the artistic
beauty of metaphors and parables to help
you understand God's kingdom. However,
beware of using such artistic language to
construct doctrines.

5. *Interrogate each passage and make sure you are
   noticing everything it has to say.* Ask yourself
   the following questions: Who? What?
   Where? When? Why? How? Slow down and
   ask the questions, and you'll be surprised at
   how much more you learn.

6. *Look for relationships between ideas.* If/then
   phrases and words like "therefore" will help
   you track with the arguments being made
   in the passage. Sometimes they indicate
   important conditions imposed on specific
   promises. Pay attention!

7. *Determine who is speaking.* You can't treat
   every statement as a statement from God.
   Some of the passages in the Bible are the

words of the devil or untrustworthy men and
women. Also, don't assume that because the
psalmist expresses a strong emotion about
something (like hatred for his enemies)
that such a statement represents how God
feels. Carefully differentiate between what
God actually says and what His imperfect
followers say.

8. *Pay attention to the literary genre.* Poetry,
history, narrative, parables, and apocalyptic
passages all have their own rules of
interpretation. It's worth learning a little
about these.

9. *Let Scripture interpret Scripture.* The best
way to check for the accuracy of your
interpretation is to compare it with other
passages on the same topic.

10. *What you focus on determines what you miss,
so read the Scriptures again and again, each
time trying to focus on something different.*
I have a friend who had read the books of

the minor prophets numerous times over the years, but one day realized that he had failed to see what they taught about social justice because he was too busy looking for prophecies about the end times.

11. *Don't be afraid to consult commentaries and reference tools.* There are many great scholars who can provide information that you'll probably never discover on your own—the original meanings of words, historical background, cultural idiosyncrasies, and how the passages fit into the overall theological development of the Bible. Don't be too proud to ask for help from the experts.

12. *Push forward to practical application.* Don't settle for simply reading the Bible as a theological text. Read it, but also ask yourself how the passage applies to your life and what you need to do about it. How should it change the way you think and change the way you live?

A NINETY-DAY BIBLE HIGHLIGHTS READING PLAN

If you've never read the Bible before—or maybe just read a little here and there—this plan will provide a good overview of the most famous passages of the Bible in only three months' time. By reading just one chapter a day, you'll hit most of the highlights: the memorable stories, the beautiful poetry, and the life-changing teaching. After that you'll be ready to explore the whole Bible, chapter by chapter. You'll find lots of treasure just waiting to be discovered!

❏ Day 1–Genesis 1

❏ Day 2–Genesis 2

❏ Day 3–Genesis 3

❏ Day 4–Genesis 6

❏ Day 5–Genesis 7

❏ Day 6–Genesis 8

❏ Day 7–Genesis 12

❏ Day 8–Genesis 32

❏ Day 9–Genesis 37

❏ Day 10–Exodus 3

❏ Day 11–Exodus 12

❏ Day 12–Exodus 14

❏ Day 13–Numbers 20

❏ Day 14–Deuteronomy 1

❏ Day 15–Deuteronomy 5

❏ Day 16–Deuteronomy 6

❑ Day 55–Matthew 6

❑ Day 56–Matthew 7

❑ Day 57–Matthew 24

❑ Day 58–Matthew 28

❑ Day 59–Mark 4

❑ Day 60–Luke 2

❑ Day 61–Luke 15

❑ Day 62–Luke 24

❑ Day 63–John 1

❑ Day 64–John 3

❑ Day 65–John 10

❑ Day 66–John 14

❑ Day 67–John 15

❑ Day 68–John 17

❑ Day 69–Acts 2

❑ Day 70–Acts 9

❑ Day 71–Romans 3

❑ Day 72–Romans 6

❑ Day 73–Romans 8

❑ Day 74–Romans 12

❑ Day 75–
1 Corinthians 13

❑ Day 76–Galatians 5

❑ Day 77–Ephesians 1

❑ Day 78–Ephesians 5

❑ Day 79–Ephesians 6

❑ Day 80–Philippians 2

❑ Day 81–Colossians 2

❑ Day 82–
1 Thessalonians 4

❑ Day 83–2 Timothy 3

❑ Day 84–Hebrews 11

❑ Day 85–James 2

❑ Day 86–1 John 2

❑ Day 87–1 John 3

❑ Day 88–Revelation 4

❑ Day 89–Revelation 21

❑ Day 90–Revelation 22

Part Two

A Quick Tour
of the Bible

A FIVE-MINUTE OVERVIEW OF THE ENTIRE BIBLE

The events of the Bible can be grouped into a few chronological eras to help capture the overall flow of the biblical story. There's no way to give an adequate summary in such a short amount of space, but here's the big picture.

The Era of Creation and Early History (Genesis 1–11). The Bible begins by telling us how the world came into existence and how human beings became separated from their original innocent relationship with God. It records the first murder, the origin of languages and nations (the Tower of Babel), and the flood, which God used to bring judgment on the people who had turned away from Him.

The Era of the Patriarchs (Genesis 12–50 and possibly the book of Job). Abraham, a nomad, was chosen to begin a lineage of people who were to be God's own chosen people to do God's will on the earth. Abraham's grandson Jacob was renamed "Israel" after an experience of wrestling with God. Jacob's twelve sons eventually formed the twelve tribes of Israel and later settled in Egypt to avoid famine, but they eventually became slaves in the land.

The Era of the Exodus and Wanderings (Exodus–Joshua). God called Moses to lead the people out of Egypt and into the promised land. Due to their disobedience, the Israelites spent 40 years wandering in the wilderness before they finally conquered the land under the leadership of Joshua.

The Era of the Judges (Judges). God provided wise judges to lead the people of Israel during these dark days of Jewish history when there was a cyclical pattern of idolatry and immorality. Just when things began to improve, the people would fall back into the practice of idolatry, and things would take a turn for the worst! This pattern repeated itself again and again.

~

The Era of the Kings (1 Samuel–2 Chronicles, as well as Psalms, Proverbs, Ecclesiastes, Song of Solomon, and some of the books of the prophets). Despite the advice of the prophet Samuel, the people pleaded for a king. King Saul, the first king, was largely a failure. Following him were the reigns of David and Solomon, the high points of the monarchy. The deterioration of Israel was rapid under the reigns of Solomon's sons. Israel was split into two kingdoms: the northern kingdom of Israel and the southern kingdom of Judah. Both kingdoms suffered greatly from poor leadership and sank into idolatry and immorality.

~

The Era of Exile and Return (Ezra–Nehemiah and some of the books of the prophets). The people of Israel and Judah were taken into captivity by the Babylonians. They were not allowed to return to their land until some 70 years later when the temple and the city of Jerusalem were both restored and rebuilt.

The Era of Silence. There is a 400-year gap between the end of the Old Testament and the beginning of the New Testament. Toward the end of this period, the Jews lived under Roman rule.

The Era of Jesus Christ (Matthew–John). God Himself entered history in the person of Jesus Christ to fulfill the promise of Israel and invite Gentiles into the kingdom of God. Jesus taught, performed miracles, and was crucified on a cross. He rose from the dead for the salvation of mankind.

The Era of the Early Church (Acts–Revelation). Through the work of the Holy Spirit, Jesus empowered His disciples to carry on His message and establish the church, which would serve as His "body" on the earth. The latter books of the New Testament are letters addressing problems in the church and providing Christians with instructions on how to live *in* Christ. They also encourage Christians to look forward to the time when Jesus would come again.

A GUIDED TOUR OF THE BIBLE, BOOK BY BOOK

The Old Testament

GENESIS

Genesis is the book of beginnings, a book that provides answers for the big questions people have always asked. *Where did we come from? Why are we here? Why is there so much evil and suffering in the world?* Genesis does not answer these questions in the way we'd usually expect— through some sort of philosophical or theological discourse—but rather, through telling stories about God's relationship with His people.

Included are the story of Creation, the story of the Fall, the story of Noah and the great flood, and the stories of Abraham, Isaac, Jacob, and Joseph. Thus begins the story of God's plan to redeem humanity. Structurally, the first eleven chapters cover a long period of time (starting with the very beginning). In the latter chapters, the pace slows down and the focus is on God's interaction with Abraham and his descendants, who become God's chosen people.

Some Key Moments in Genesis:

- The Creation *(Genesis 1–2)*
- The fall of humanity *(Genesis 3)*
- Noah and the flood *(Genesis 6–8)*
- The Tower of Babel *(Genesis 11)*
- The call of Abraham *(Genesis 12)*
- Sodom and Gomorrah *(Genesis 18–19)*
- Jacob wrestles with the angel *(Genesis 32)*

EXODUS

By the conclusion of the book of Genesis, the chosen people are in Egypt, and over time they eventually become captives, slaves of the Egyptians. But Moses obeys a call from God to lead his people out of captivity and to Mt. Sinai.

There God gives them the Law; instructions in how they are to live as the chosen people of God.

Some Key Moments in Exodus:

- God speaks to Moses out of the burning bush *(Exodus 3)*
- The plagues and the escape from Egypt *(Exodus 7–14)*
- The Ten Commandments *(Exodus 20)*
- The golden calf *(Exodus 32)*

The Ten Commandments:

1. *You shall have no other gods before me.*
2. *You shall not make for yourself an idol in the form of anything in heaven above or on the earth beneath…*
3. *You shall not misuse the name of the LORD your God…*
4. *Remember the Sabbath day by keeping it holy.*
5. *Honor your father and your mother…*
6. *You shall not murder.*

7. *You shall not commit adultery.*

8. *You shall not steal.*

9. *You shall not give false testimony against your neighbor.*

10. *You shall not covet…*

～

LEVITICUS

With Leviticus we turn to the rule book of the Old Testament. And let's be honest. It isn't quite the action/adventure story that parts of Genesis and Exodus are. But Leviticus serves an important function for God's people. It is filled with advice and commandments on how to live and how to worship God.

In addition to the expected laws about morality, this book deals with the system of offerings, ritual purity, and the priesthood. Along the way there are guidelines for what to eat, what to do about skin disease, how to treat the poor and the needy, and much more. Some of the laws seem strange to us today, but in the context of the time, they helped people lead lives of health and harmony.

Some Key Moments in Leviticus:

- The first priests *(Leviticus 8)*
- The holy days and festivals *(Leviticus 23)*

NUMBERS

Unless you are a numbers person, you might find this book to be rather tedious. There is a lot of counting happening in these pages, a sort of biblical census. But that's not all. In a sense, you can think of this book as the story of Plan B, the years of wandering in the wilderness brought on by Israel's disobedience. The chosen ones are on their way to the promised land, but there are many struggles along the path.

Some Key Moments in Numbers:

- The spies and their report *(Numbers 13–14)*

- Moses' disobedience *(Numbers 20)*
- Balaam and the donkey *(Numbers 22)*
- Joshua appointed as leader *(Numbers 27)*

DEUTERONOMY

Deuteronomy is the transcription of Moses' farewell sermons, his last words to his people before his death. Because he will not be entering the promised land with them, Moses wishes to remind them of their covenant relationship with God. Due to who God has made them through this covenant, the Lord requires nothing less than complete allegiance. Deuteronomy emphasizes the idea that God's laws are the result of God's love.

Some Key Moments in Deuteronomy:

- The Ten Commandments restated
  (Deuteronomy 5)

- Moses teaches about God's love
  (Deuteronomy 6–7)
- God's concern for the poor and needy
  (Deuteronomy 15)
- The last days and death of Moses
  (Deuteronomy 32–34)

JOSHUA

After all their years of wandering, the Israelites are finally able to enter the promised land. However, before they can claim what God has promised them, they must wage battles against a number of enemies. This is a book of violence and high drama as the land is taken, piece-by-piece, under the leadership of Joshua. Once they have taken the land, it is divided between the twelve tribes of Israel.

Some Key Moments in Joshua:

- Rahab and the spies *(Joshua 2)*

- The battle of Jericho *(Joshua 6)*
- The sun stands still during battle *(Joshua 10)*

JUDGES

Judges contains some great stories, but it is generally a pretty depressing read. Following the death of Joshua, God raises up a series of judges to rule the land. A cyclical pattern emerges—over and over again, the people disobey God and bring violence and shame upon their land. The recurring phrase is "everyone did as he saw fit."

They selfishly followed their own path, a path which led to defeat and destruction rather than what God had in mind for them. Judges is a testimony to the infinite patience of God—He continued sending new leaders for the people even though they made the same mistakes time and again!

Some Key Moments in Judges:

- Deborah, the first woman judge *(Judges 4–5)*

- The story of Gideon *(Judges 6–8)*
- The story of Samson *(Judges 13–16)*

RUTH

After all the violence and disobedience recorded in Judges, the book of Ruth is a breath of fresh air, a gentle tale of love and redemption. It is interesting that Ruth, the heroine of this story, is not an Israelite, but a Moabite—a member of one of the nations that was an enemy of Israel. This adds even more poignancy to this unforgettable story of friendship, loyalty, kindness, and real love.

A Key Moment in Ruth:

- The kinsman-redeemer *(Ruth 3)*

FIRST SAMUEL

First Samuel deals with the beginnings of the Israelite monarchy. It revolves around three men: Samuel, the faithful prophet; Saul, the troubled and often disobedient first king; and David, Saul's successor. Up to this time, God had been considered Israel's king, but now the people of Israel wanted a human king. In a time of great national disaster, Samuel calls for spiritual renewal, and despite the warnings God had given, the people demand a king. So Saul is anointed king but proves himself a failure.

In his last great act as God's prophet, Samuel anoints David, a young shepherd boy, to be his successor. After young David shows himself a hero in combat by defeating the seemingly unbeatable enemy soldier, Goliath, Saul's jealousy grows and his downhill slide begins—ending with his suicide on the battlefield.

Some Key Moments in First Samuel:

- The people demand a king *(1 Samuel 8)*
- David and Goliath *(1 Samuel 17)*
- David and Jonathan *(1 Samuel 18–20)*

SECOND SAMUEL

The narrative of the early Israelite monarchy continues with David's reign following the death of Saul. At first highly successful, David manages to unite all of Israel under his rule and establishes Jerusalem as the capital. His own moral failures come to the forefront when he becomes involved with Bathsheba. Later, he nearly loses his throne in a plot hatched by his own son, Absalom.

Some Key Moments in Second Samuel:

- David and Bathsheba *(2 Samuel 11–12)*
- The death of Absalom *(2 Samuel 18)*

FIRST KINGS

First Kings was most likely written during the exile of Israel in Babylon. It is a narrative answer to the nagging questions: What went wrong? How does Israel plummet from the good years it knew with kings David and Solomon to the despair that followed as the nation became enslaved in a foreign land?

The book begins with the death of David and chronicles the reign of Solomon. Solomon builds the temple (an astonishing work of ancient architecture) and expands the power of the nation. But Solomon, usually known for his wisdom, fails to show much of it when choosing his wives. Several of his wives come from neighboring nations and introduce the kingdom to the worship of other gods. Wisdom is obviously not genetic because Solomon's sons bring disaster and Israel is divided into two kingdoms: Israel in the north and Judah in the south. Although God sends prophets to try to help the people, what follows is a succession of predominantly bad kings.

Some Key Moments in First Kings:

- The wisdom of Solomon *(1 Kings 3–4)*
- Solomon and the Queen of Sheba *(1 Kings 10)*
- The kingdom divided *(1 Kings 12)*
- Ahab and Jezebel *(1 Kings 16–22)*
- Elijah and the prophets of Baal *(1 Kings 18)*

~

SECOND KINGS

Originally part of the same scroll as First Kings, this book continues the unfortunate story of the decline and fall of Israel. Despite a few bright years of repentance and spiritual renewal under King Josiah, first Israel and then Judah spiral downward into idolatry under the rule of evil kings. The book ends with the eventual destruction of the nation and exile of the people into a foreign land.

Some Key Moments in Second Kings:

- Elijah transported to heaven *(2 Kings 2)*
- The ministry of Elisha *(2 Kings 2–6)*
- Josiah's reforms *(2 Kings 22–23)*
- Northern kingdom of Israel destroyed
  (2 Kings 17)
- Southern kingdom of Judah destroyed
  (2 Kings 25)

FIRST CHRONICLES

Most likely written just after the Israelites' return from captivity, First Chronicles tells the same stories as Second Samuel—think of them as coming from a different "camera angle." Here the emphasis is placed more on the religious history than the political history. Much of the focus is on David's line and the southern kingdom of Judah. As such, it is a somewhat more sanitized version, offering a generally positive spin on the events and people involved. The chronicler, probably intending to unite the returning exiles with a more hopeful spin on their past, omits the stories that demonstrate David's failings.

Some Key Moments in First Chronicles:

- David becomes king *(1 Chronicles 11)*
- David's prayer for the temple *(1 Chronicles 29)*

SECOND CHRONICLES

Second Chronicles continues the story of the Davidic monarchy by recording Solomon's triumphant architectural project—building the temple. The writer, however, cannot ignore Judah's many evil kings and how their idolatry and wickedness led to the fall of David's kingdom, so he includes those stories as well.

Some Key Moments in Second Chronicles:

- Jehoshaphat as king *(2 Chronicles 17–20)*
- Hezekiah's reforms *(2 Chronicles 29–32)*
- Josiah as king *(2 Chronicles 34–35)*

A CHART OF THE KINGS AND PROPHETS OF ISRAEL AND JUDAH

(Dates are approximate and represent the general consensus.)

Date (BC)	Kings of Judah	Prophets	Kings of Israel
975	1. Rehoboam, 17 years	Ahijah	1. Jeroboam, 22 years
958	2. Abijah, 3 years	Shemaiah	
955	3. Asa, 41 years	Azariah	
954			2. Nadab, 2 years
953		Hanani	3. Baasha, 24 years
930		Jehu	4. Elah, 2 years
929			5. Zimri, 7 days
929			6. Omri, 12 years
918		Elijah	7. Ahab, 22 years
914	4. Jehoshaphat, 25 years	Micaiah	
897		Elisha	8. Ahaziah, 2 years
896		Jahaziel	9. Jehoram, 12 years

Date (BC)	Kings of Judah	Prophets	Kings of Israel
892	5. Jehoram, 8 years		
885	6. Ahaziah, 1 year		
884	Athaliah, 7 years*	Jehoiada	10. Jehu, 28 years
878	7. Joash, 40 years		
856		Jonah	11. Jehoahaz, 17 years
839	8. Amaziah, 29 years		12. Jehoash, 16 years
825		Hosea	13. Jeroboam II, 41 years
810	9. Uzziah, 52 years	Joel	Interregnum, 11 years
784		Amos	14. Zechariah, 6 months
772			15. Shallum, 1 month
771			16. Menahem, 10 years

* She usurped the throne and is not considered a legal ruler.

Date (BC)	Kings of Judah	Prophets	Kings of Israel
760			17. Pekahiah, 2 years
758			18. Pekah, 20 years
757	10. Jotham, 16 years		
741	11. Ahaz, 16 years	Obed	
730		Isaiah	19. Hoshea, 9 years
726	12. Hezekiah, 29 years	Micah	
721		Nahum	Captivity of Israel
697	13. Manasseh, 55 years	Habakkuk	
642	14. Amon, 2 years		
640	15. Josiah, 31 years	Jeremiah	
609	16. Jehoahaz, 3 months	Zephaniah	
609	17. Jehoiakim, 11 years		

Date (BC)	Kings of Judah	Prophets	Kings of Israel
606	First Captivity of Judah	Ezekiel and Daniel	
598	18. Jehoiachin, 3 months		
598	Second Captivity of Judah		
586	Last Captivity of Judah		
536	Return of Jewish Captives		
516	Temple Restored	Zechariah and Haggai	

EZRA

Ezra is the story of the return of God's people from exile in Babylon. Under Zerubbabel's leadership a fairly modest contingent returns and begins rebuilding the temple in Jerusalem. Then Ezra, a priest, returns with a much larger group and restores worship in the temple.

A Key Moment in Ezra:

- The temple is completed *(Ezra 6)*

NEHEMIAH

Nehemiah continues the story of the return from exile some 12 years after the end of Ezra. Nehemiah, a man of prayer, leads the people in restoring social justice and spiritual commitment. He guides them in rebuilding the walls of Jerusalem. After a national revival spurred by the reading of God's law, the people resettle the land.

Some Key Moments in Nehemiah:

- Rebuilding the walls *(Nehemiah 4–6)*
- Reading of the Law and confession of sin *(Nehemiah 8–9)*

ESTHER

Although God is not mentioned by name even once in the entire book of Esther, He is obviously operating behind the scenes to strengthen the resolve of Esther, a woman who uses integrity and intelligence to save her nation. It is a story of court intrigue and evil machinations with lots of danger and suspense. It is also a fairy-tale-like story of a princess who finds a way to rescue her people from an evil plot. And finally, it is the story of the origin of the feast of Purim, the only non-Mosaic feast in the Jewish calendar. (The story probably takes place during the time period covered by the book of Ezra.)

Some Key Moments in Esther:

- Esther's courageous stand *(Esther 4)*
- The institution of the feast of Purim *(Esther 9)*

∽

JOB

With Job we begin the section of Old Testament books usually referred to as the Wisdom Books. We don't know much about the historical setting of Job, but we do know that it is a brutally honest, poetic examination of suffering. If you look to the book for an answer to the problem of evil, you'll probably find it unsatisfactory. In fact, much of the book seems to focus on the inadequacy of simplistic theological answers as demonstrated by the words of Job's friends, who try to help him understand why such great evil has befallen him. Instead, the only answer to the question "why?" seems to be that we will never understand the mystery and must trust in God's wisdom and power. Ultimately the act of God speaking to Job seems answer enough for the humbled sufferer.

Some Key Moments in Job:

- The testing of Job *(Job 1–2)*
- The Lord speaks to Job *(Job 38–41)*
- Job's confession and restoration *(Job 42)*

PSALMS

Psalms is the songbook of the Bible, a collection of unforgettable hymns and songs by David, Moses, and other writers. It has been used in Jewish and Christian worship throughout the ages because the psalmists put the feelings of God's people into words and songs. And interestingly enough, there is a psalm to fit just about any mood one might be experiencing: awestruck reverence, impatience with God, anger with and fear of your enemies, and cries for help. The book of Psalms is filled with raw human emotion and beautiful poetic expression, making it a favorite of many Bible readers.

Psalms—The Greatest Hits
(some of the most popular psalms):

The results of meditating on God's Word *(Psalm 1)*

A psalm of praise to the Creator *(Psalm 8)*

A psalm of trust, even in the face of death *(Psalm 13)*

"The heavens declare the glory of God…" *(Psalm19)*

A lament of pain that prophetically echoes Jesus' experience on the cross *(Psalm 22)*

"The Lord is my shepherd…" *(Psalm 23)*

A psalm of confident trust in God *(Psalm 27)*

A beautifully poetic plea for deliverance and hope *(Psalm 42)*

A psalm of confession and forgiveness written following David's sin with Bathsheba *(Psalm 51)*

A psalm of jubilation in difficult times *(Psalm 89)*

A psalm expressing peace in the midst of fear *(Psalm 91)*

A psalm of praise and thanksgiving *(Psalm 100)*

A hymn of praise drawing upon the creation story *(Psalm 104)*

The longest psalm, it is a celebration of the Word of God *(Psalm 119)*

A psalm reminding us that God knows us intimately *(Psalm 139)*

A psalm of unbridled worship and praise *(Psalm 150)*

PROVERBS

Proverbs is a collection of wise sayings by Solomon and others. It contains practical advice in memorable, bite-size snippets on such topics as the need for wisdom, the danger of bad companions, the requirement of being compassionate toward the needy, the dangers posed by the tongue, the hazards of sexual immorality, and the foolishness of the lazy. Its overall theme is this: The fear of the Lord is the beginning of wisdom.

A Handful of Favorite Proverbs:

Trust in the LORD with all your heart and lean not on your own understanding; in all your ways acknowledge him, and he will make your paths straight. (Proverbs 3:5-6)

How long will you lie there, you sluggard? When will you get up from your sleep? A little sleep, a little slumber, a little folding of the hands to rest— and poverty will come on you like a bandit and scarcity like an armed man. (Proverbs 6:9-11)

There are six things the LORD hates, seven that are detestable to him: haughty eyes, a lying tongue, hands that shed innocent blood, a heart that devises wicked schemes, feet that are quick to rush into evil, a false witness who pours out lies, and a man who stirs up dissension among brothers. (Proverbs 6:16-19)

Do not rebuke a mocker or he will hate you; rebuke a wise man and he will love you. Instruct a wise man and he will be wiser still; teach a righteous man and he will add to his learning. (Proverbs 9:8-9)

The fear of the LORD is the beginning of wisdom... (Proverbs 9:10)

Like a gold ring in a pig's snout is a beautiful woman who shows no discretion. (Proverbs 11:22)

He who guards his lips guards his life, but he who speaks rashly will come to ruin. (Proverbs 13:3)

A patient man has great understanding, but a quick-tempered man displays folly. (Proverbs 14:29)

A gentle answer turns away wrath, but a harsh word stirs up anger. (Proverbs 15:1)

He who mocks the poor shows contempt for their Maker; whoever gloats over disaster will not go unpunished. (Proverbs 17:5)

A word aptly spoken is like apples of gold in settings of silver. (Proverbs 25:11)

Like one who seizes a dog by the ears is a passer-by who meddles in a quarrel not his own. (Proverbs 26:17)

Let another praise you, and not your own mouth; someone else, and not your own lips. (Proverbs 27:2)

Charm is deceptive, and beauty is fleeting; but a woman who fears the LORD is to be praised. (Proverbs 31:30)

ECCLESIASTES

Ecclesiastes confirms that being a person of faith does not always mean being a positive thinker! This book is an honest and open-eyed philosophical reflection on life…and the conclusions are pretty negative. Everywhere the author of Ecclesiastes looks, he sees examples of life's apparent lack of meaning—inequality and unfairness, religious hypocrisy, and the uncertainty of the future. But under all the vanity resides a deeper truth: A life lived with and for God gives us meaning, wisdom, and purpose, even if it doesn't guarantee that everything is always going to come up roses.

Some Key Moments in Ecclesiastes:

- The apparent pointlessness of life *(Ecclesiastes 1)*
- A time for everything *(Ecclesiastes 3)*
- Serve God while you are young *(Ecclesiastes 11–12)*

SONG OF SOLOMON
(also known as Song of Songs)

Those who equate sin with sexuality may be surprised to find this book in the Bible. It is an unabashed and earthy celebration of romance, filled with two lovers' poetic descriptions of their longings and unquenchable desires for one another. Here is the joy of married love as God originally intended it! (Some also see this poem as an allegory of God's love for Israel and Christ's love for the Church. It certainly can be read that way, but don't miss recognizing how it celebrates love between a man and woman.)

Some Key Moments in the Song of Solomon:

- Description of the bride *(Song of Solomon 4)*
- Description of the groom *(Song of Solomon 5)*

ISAIAH

Isaiah was a prophet in Judah during the reigns of four kings, and his primary message was to warn each king of the threat posed by Assyria and Babylonia. But in the midst of those dire threats of judgment, he also gave a message of future hope, looking beyond the immediate future and into the reign of the coming Messiah.

Isaiah is one of the most beautifully written books of the Bible, filled with powerful images and memorable phrases. The main theme of Isaiah is not only judgment of Judah and its enemies, but ultimately that salvation comes from God alone.

Some Key Moments in Isaiah:
- The call of Isaiah *(Isaiah 6)*
- The suffering servant *(Isaiah 53)*
- The glory of the coming kingdom *(Isaiah 65)*

JEREMIAH

Poor Jeremiah—he preached, but no one seemed to be listening. Jeremiah prophesied in Jerusalem, warning of the impending punishment of Judah. He is known as the "weeping prophet" for the emotional tone of his dire predictions and because of the great sacrifices he made to preach his message. Throughout his entire career, Jeremiah received no positive response, as though he was preaching into the wind. But he persevered in the face of frustration and pointed toward the Potter (God) who wished to shape the clay (His people) into what He intended for them.

Some Key Moments in Jeremiah:

- The potter and the clay *(Jeremiah 18)*
- The new covenant *(Jeremiah 31)*

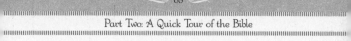

LAMENTATIONS

Traditionally thought to be the work of the prophet Jeremiah, Lamentations is filled with the cries of physical and spiritual agony brought on by the consequences of sin—abandoning God's ways. At the time Jerusalem lay in ruins at the hand of its enemies.

The book, much of it set out as an elaborate acrostic in Hebrew, is a prayer of lament. It is both a calling upon the people to repent and submit to God and a calling upon God for forgiveness and for vindication against the enemies of God's people. The book reminds us that a cry of despair over misfortune and suffering is a valid form of prayer!

A Key Moment in Lamentations:

- A reminder of God's faithfulness

   (Lamentations 3)

EZEKIEL

Ezekiel was God's "performance artist." It wasn't enough for him to preach to the exiles in Babylon; he was given the job of enacting a series of odd parables to help his fellow Israelites see the truth and look forward to God's salvation. He ate a scroll—yes, ate it. He lay on his side for 390 days. Then on his other side for many more days. Ezekiel ate only one meal a day...cooked over manure. He smashed pottery and spoke of the fantastical symbolic visions that God had given him. To many Ezekiel might have seemed crazy, but his message was one of visionary hope.

Some Key Moments in Ezekiel:

- A vision of God's glory *(Ezekiel 1)*
- The valley of dry bones *(Ezekiel 37)*
- The future heavenly temple *(Ezekiel 40–48)*

DANIEL

Daniel contains some of the most interesting stories in all the books of the prophets and also some of the most head-scratching prophetic visions—a fascinating book of strong faith in action and predictions of the future. Daniel was an exiled Jew living in Babylon who resisted the temptation to accommodate a pagan culture. His wisdom and godly character earned him respect and favor.

Some Key Moments in Daniel:

- Nebuchadnezzar's dream and its interpretation *(Daniel 2)*
- The fiery furnace *(Daniel 3)*
- Belshazzar's feast *(Daniel 5)*
- Daniel in the lion's den *(Daniel 6)*
- Daniel's prophecy of the 70 years *(Daniel 9)*

HOSEA

The story of the prophet Hosea is a lived-out illustration of God's infinite patience and love for His people. Hosea, who was a prophet in Israel, is commanded to do something very unexpected—marry a known prostitute and have children with her. He does, but the marriage quickly deteriorates. She commits adultery, an unfaithfulness that parallels Israel's unfaithfulness to God.

Hosea does not give up on his wife. His patient love for her is a reminder of how God feels about His people. But that doesn't mean they don't need a stern rebuke for their moral depravity, apostasy, and idolatry. Love sometimes demands calling for repentance.

Some Key Moments in Hosea:

- Hosea and Gomer *(Hosea 1–3)*
- A hopeful future *(Hosea 14)*

JOEL

The prophet Joel's message is that judgment precedes revival. When a plague of locusts descends upon Judah, Joel explains that this is just a foretaste of the coming day of the Lord when great judgment will come upon all people... unless they humble themselves and repent.

A Key Moment in Joel:

• The events of the day of the Lord *(Joel 2)*

AMOS

Amos was a plain-spoken shepherd who, though his home was in Judah, crossed over into Israel to preach. He had strong words of condemnation for Israel's smug, self-satisfied religiosity and their flirtation with idolatry. God, Amos declared, hates false religion. He also spoke out against the corruption of Jewish society and the injustice that left the poor forgotten and oppressed. God, he reminded Israel, will not tolerate such neglect.

A Key Moment in Amos:

• A warning to the self-indulgent rich *(Amos 6)*

OBADIAH

Obadiah is the shortest book of the Old Testament—only one chapter long. Its theme is the coming destruction of Edom (a neighboring nation) due to its wickedness and cruelty. Scholars are not sure where it fits into the chronology of Jewish history, but it seems likely that Obadiah was a contemporary of Elisha.

JONAH

The story of Jonah and the big fish (the Bible doesn't say it was a whale!) is one of the most familiar Bible stories, but there is more to this book than just that tale. It also provides us with the message that God's love extends beyond His chosen people to encompass everyone.

After Jonah's incident with the big fish, which follows his attempt to evade God's call to go and preach repentance to Nineveh, his preaching is successful. They repent, they mourn their sin, and God spares Nineveh from His judgment. When Jonah is angered that these pagans have been shown God's mercy, God rebukes Jonah and reveals His intention to offer grace and mercy to all people.

A Key Moment in Jonah:
• Jonah and the big fish *(Jonah 1–2)*

MICAH

The prophet Micah speaks out against the social injustice in Israel and Samaria. He points to their oppression of the poor by the rich, the hypocrisy of the national and religious leaders, and their spiritual bankruptcy. It is a clear demonstration that God desires more than just personal holiness, but also social righteousness and justice. To that end Micah gives a prophetic glimpse of the glorious future when the Lord will regather His people in a kingdom ruled by the Messiah.

A Key Moment in Micah:

• Judgment upon the oppressors of the poor
   (Micah 3)

NAHUM

A contemporary of Jeremiah and Zephaniah, Nahum predicts the judgment of Nineveh (some 125 years after Jonah's missionary trip via the big fish). The people had returned to their old ways! The God who is slow to anger, declares Nahum, has finally had it with Nineveh's (and all of Assyria's) evil ways.

A Key Moment in Nahum:

• A psalm of God's majesty *(Nahum 1)*

HABAKKUK

It was a dark time in Judah. A time of violence and corruption, injustice and neglect, and much suffering. And there, on the horizon, was lurking the invasion by Babylonia. In the midst of all this conflict, Habakkuk struggles with the question of why God was allowing this to happen. The form of the book is a conversation between the prophet and the Lord. Habakkuk asks the question, "Why did you allow this?" God's answer is simple—judgment upon the corrupt leaders of Judah. But are the Babylonians any better? No. God reveals that they too will be judged. The book ends with Habakkuk's prayer of faith and trust.

A Key Moment in Habakkuk:

• The righteous will live by faith *(Habakkuk 2)*

ZEPHANIAH

Zephaniah was a distant member of the royal family who prophesied during the early reign of Josiah. He assured the people that Judah would be judged and looked toward the coming day of the Lord. Since Josiah became a good king, Zephaniah's message appears to have gotten through!

HAGGAI

Haggai was a Jewish exile who returned to Jerusalem with the second wave of returnees. He found the morale of Jerusalem's citizens to be very low. Life was so difficult that the temple rebuilding project had been temporarily abandoned. Haggai reminds the people that the temple is more than just a building, but a sign that the land will be rededicated to God. This means putting God first—then they (we) will experience His blessings.

A Key Moment in Haggai:

- The prophecy of the temple *(Haggai 2)*

ZECHARIAH

Like his contemporary Haggai, Zechariah was preaching to the discouraged Jews who had returned from exile in Babylon. But instead of focusing on the present as Haggai was doing, Zechariah had a series of eight strange visions of the future. There is no scholarly agreement on the precise meaning of these visions, but it is clear that much of it concerns Zechariah's prophetic predictions of the coming Messiah, Jesus. And when he is speaking of this glorious future, he can barely contain his excitement.

A Key Moment in Zechariah:

- The wounded shepherd and the redemption of Israel *(Zechariah 12–13)*

MALACHI

Probably the last prophet of the Old Testament times, Malachi speaks to those who have returned from exile about staying true to God's ways. In those tough times, it was easy to neglect responsibilities to God and His temple and become spiritually stagnant. Beware of falsehood and neglect, he says, and stay true to God and follow His ways.

A Key Moment in Malachi:

- The people's sin against God *(Malachi 3)*

The New Testament

❧

MATTHEW

Matthew is the first of the four Gospels, though it most likely was not the first to be written—that distinction belongs to Mark. Matthew, more than the other three Gospels, looks at the life and death of Jesus from a Jewish perspective, connecting these events with the hopes and expectations of the Jews. Thus, Matthew provides a genealogy that demonstrates Jesus' royal heritage and tries to connect the events of Jesus' life with the fulfillment of Old Testament prophecies. He quotes the Old Testament to prove the point he wishes to make clear to his readers: Jesus of Nazareth is the longed-for Messiah, the One who ushers in the kingdom of God.

Some Key Moments in Matthew:

• The birth of Jesus *(Mattew 1–2)*

- The Sermon on the Mount *(Matthew 5–7)*

- Prophecies of the last days *(Matthew 24)*

- The parable of the sheep and the goats
  (Matthew 25)

- The resurrection of Jesus *(Matthew 28)*

The Beatitudes (Matthew 5:3-10)

Blessed are the poor in spirit, for theirs is the kingdom of heaven.

Blessed are those who mourn, for they will be comforted.

Blessed are the meek, for they will inherit the earth.

Blessed are those who hunger and thirst for righteousness, for they will be filled.

Blessed are the merciful, for they will be shown mercy.

Blessed are the pure in heart, for they will see God.

Blessed are the peacemakers, for they will be called sons of God.

Blessed are those who are persecuted because of righteousness, for theirs is the kingdom of heaven.

~

MARK

Mark is the earliest of the Gospels, and it is also the shortest and fastest paced. Mark doesn't worry about explaining Jesus' lineage or the details of His birth. He just jumps right into recounting the ministry of Jesus during the three years before His death. Amidst all the action though, Mark stops now and then to explain various Jewish customs that pertain to the story, which leads us to believe that he is writing for a non-Jewish audience, probably Roman citizens. The Romans always loved a man of action!

Some Key Moments in Mark:

- The terrible fate of John the Baptist *(Mark 6)*

- Jesus walks on water *(Mark 6)*
- The cost of following Jesus *(Mark 10)*
- The last days *(Mark 13)*

LUKE

Luke's intentions are made clear in the very first few verses of his Gospel: to tell the story of Jesus with an eye for careful accuracy and research, producing a trustworthy account of what really happened. His audience, as with Mark, was the Gentiles, and Luke was likely a Gentile himself. He recounts the story of the universal Savior, not just for the Jews, but for all people. Luke gives a lot of attention to the teaching of Jesus, particularly the parables. And he also shows a deep recognition for Jesus' concern for the outcasts of society: the poor, the downtrodden, the sick, and the suffering. To them Jesus brings a message of hope and the love of a heavenly Father.

Some Key Moments in Luke:

- The birth of Jesus *(Luke 1–2)*
- The parable of the good Samaritan *(Luke 10)*
- Teaching on prayer *(Luke 11)*
- The parable of the prodigal son *(Luke 15)*

THE MAJOR PARABLES OF JESUS AND WHERE TO FIND THEM

The wise and foolish builders *(Matthew 7:24-27; Luke 6:47-49)*

The sower and the seeds *(Matthew 13:3-8,18-23; Mark 4:3-8, 14-20; Luke 8:5-8,11-15)*

The pearl of great price *(Matthew 13:45-46)*

The lost sheep *(Matthew 18:12-14; Luke 15:4-7)*

The unmerciful servant *(Matthew 18:23-34)*

The workers in the vineyard *(Matthew 20:1-16)*

The two sons *(Matthew 21:28-32)*

The tenants *(Matthew 21:33-44; Mark 12:1-11; Luke 20:9-18)*

The wedding banquet *(Matthew 22:2-14)*

The fig tree *(Matthew 24:32-35; Mark 13:28-29; Luke 21:29-31)*

The faithful and wise servant *(Matthew 24:45-51; Luke 12:42-48)*

The ten virgins *(Matthew 25:1-13)*

The talents *(Matthew 25:14-30; Luke 19:12-27)*

The sheep and the goats *(Matthew 25:31-46)*

The good Samaritan *(Luke 10:30-37)*

The rich fool *(Luke 12:16-21)*

The great banquet *(Luke 14:16-24)*

The lost coin *(Luke 15:8-10)*

The prodigal son *(Luke 15:11-32)*

The rich man and Lazarus *(Luke 16:19-31)*

The persistent widow *(Luke 18:2-8)*

JOHN

The first three Gospels are often referred to as the "Synoptic Gospels" due to their similarities in the events they portray, but John's Gospel is different from the others. John is more philosophical and theological, exploring the deepest mysteries of who Jesus was and why He came. The book is structured around the great signs of Jesus' divinity and the "I am" statements that Jesus utters. In many ways it is the most personally moving and spiritually challenging of the Gospels and focuses on many memorable monologues given by Jesus.

Some Key Moments in John:

- The prologue: "In the beginning was the Word" *(John 1)*
- The great "for God so loved…" statement *(John 3)*
- Jesus and the Samaritan woman *(John 4)*
- Jesus' last discourse *(John 13–17)*

• Crucifixion and resurrection *(John 19–20)*

The Great "I Am" Statements of John:

I am the Bread of Life (John 6:35,48)

I am the Light of the World (John 8:12; 9:5)

I am the Door (John 10:7,9)

I am the Good Shepherd (John 10:11,14)

I am the Resurrection and the Life (John 11:25)

I am the Way, the Truth, and the Life (John 14:6)

ACTS

In Acts Luke continues the narrative of his Gospel by sharing the story of the early church. He recounts the way the church expanded in an almost concentric manner—first Jerusalem, then Samaria, then to the ends of the earth. For the first twelve chapters, the focus is largely on Peter, though we also see the story of Stephen, the first martyr. One of those present at Stephen's death is a Pharisee named Saul. In chapter thirteen the focus of the book changes to Saul, who is converted and given a new name—Paul. The remainder of Acts deals with Paul's courageous witness throughout the Roman world to Jews and Gentiles alike.

Some Key Moments in Acts:

- The day of Pentecost and Peter's first sermon *(Acts 2)*
- Ananias and Sapphira *(Acts 5)*
- Paul's conversion *(Acts 9)*
- The council at Jerusalem *(Acts 15)*
- Paul's journey to Rome *(Acts 27–28)*

Paul's Missionary Journeys

Cyprus, Perga, Pisidian Antioch, Iconium, Lystra, and Derbe *(Acts 13:2–14:28)*

Troas, Philippi, Thessalonica, Berea, Athens, Corinth, Ephesus *(Acts 15:36–18:22)*

Ephesus, Troas, Miletus *(Acts 19:22–21:16)*

Rome *(Acts 21:17–28:31)*

ROMANS

Romans is primarily the New Testament's book of theology. This letter, written to Christians in Rome, is Paul's attempt to explain the meaning of the Gospel—that salvation is not the result of efforts or moral goodness, but solely based upon what Jesus has accomplished through His death and resurrection. The message: We are all guilty, but Jesus has become the "New Adam" and made a way for us to be restored to a relationship with God—a relationship so intimate that we may call him *Father*. Nothing, Paul reminds us, can sever us from God's love.

Some Key Moments in Romans:

- Universal sinfulness *(Romans 1–3)*
- Adam and Jesus *(Romans 5)*

- New life in Christ *(Romans 6–8)*
- Nothing can separate us from God's love *(Romans 8)*
- Living righteously *(Romans 12)*

FIRST CORINTHIANS

The church at Corinth had a lot of problems… and problems that sound familiar to us even today. It was a church marked by division, enmity, and infighting, by sexual immorality, by an unwillingness to live by God's commands, and by taking worship (especially the Lord's supper) too lightly. Paul points out that there are two kinds of Christians—the *spiritual* who live by the power of God's indwelling Spirit, and the *worldly* who simply live life by their own desires. To find true unity, meaningful worship, and moral strength, Paul reminds the Corinthians that we are all interconnected members of the body of Christ and have a variety of gifts to offer one another.

He closes the book with an emphasis on the resurrection of Christ, which is the basis for our own resurrection, our spiritual strength, and our eternal salvation.

Some Key Moments in First Corinthians:

- Sex, marriage, and divorce *(1 Corinthians 7)*
- The spiritual gifts *(1 Corinthians 12–14)*
- The primacy of love *(1 Corinthians 13)*

SECOND CORINTHIANS

Some of the recipients of Paul's earlier letter to Corinth had taken a "who are you to tell us what to do?" attitude toward the apostle. In this second letter, Paul defends his life and ministry, pointing to the way that God had honored the call upon his life with great success and fruitfulness. Speaking from experience, Paul also points out that the life of service to God sometimes results in great suffering and persecution.

A Key Moment in Second Corinthians:

- Paul's "thorn in the flesh" *(2 Corinthians 12)*

GALATIANS

Probably the earliest of Paul's letters, he deals with one of the thorniest issues to face the early church—religious legalism. Because the church arose out of Judaism, should Gentile believers be required to follow the Jewish laws and, specifically, the rite of circumcision? Paul's answer is clear and stated strongly. No. He says the gospel of Jesus is not about laws and works, but about love and faith. Through grace Christ has made us free!

Some Key Moments in Galatians:

- Justification by faith *(Galatians 2)*
- The "fruit of the Spirit" *(Galatians 5)*

EPHESIANS

Paul's letter to the Ephesians reminds the Christian that not only are we chosen and loved by God, but also empowered by the Spirit to live a new life *in* Christ. That new life is manifested in a holy lifestyle, our family relationships, and in our ability to withstand the temptations of the devil, the enemy of our souls. The letter has two neatly divided halves—the first section provides a theological understanding of how we are empowered to live as Christians, and the second gives us practical instructions for "walking in the Spirit."

Some Key Moments in Ephesians:

- Our position in Christ *(Ephesians 1)*
- Marriage and family life *(Ephesians 5–6)*
- The spiritual armor *(Ephesians 6)*

PHILIPPIANS

Philippians can best be understood as a thank-you note from Paul. While he was under house arrest, the Philippian church had not forgotten him and had sent him a gift. He expresses his appreciation and urges them to continue in the way they have begun—following Jesus with faithfulness and joy. Paul himself was an example of being joyful no matter what the circumstances.

Some Key Moments in Philippians:

- The hymn of humility *(Philippians 2)*
- Rejoicing in Christ *(Philippians 4)*

COLOSSIANS

For some people the simplicity of the Gospel is too simple! They want to find ways to make it more complicated, more intellectually exclusive. When Paul heard that such tendencies were a problem in Colossae, he sent a letter warning against an overly-intellectualized approach to faith. The Colossians had grafted a lot of mystical ideas and dietary laws onto the Gospel. Paul provides them with a strong reminder that Christianity is all about Christ…and Christ alone!

Some Key Moments in Colossians:

- The supremacy of Christ *(Colossians 1)*
- The sufficiency of Christ *(Colossians 2)*

FIRST THESSALONIANS

This is one of the most positive of Paul's letters. There is much to commend in the church at Thessalonica: their missionary zeal, their dedication to the truth, and their conduct in the world. Lest they become discouraged in the face of mounting persecution, Paul reminds them of a blessed hope—Jesus is coming again!

A Key Moment in First Thessalonians:

- The return of Christ *(1 Thessalonians 4)*

SECOND THESSALONIANS

As in the earlier letter, Paul comforts the Thessalonians with a reminder of Christ's promised return. However, he has to clear up some misunderstandings about that event because many Christians, expecting the imminent return of Jesus, had neglected to continue working to earn a living. They had built their life around waiting for the Second Coming rather than staying focused on doing the work of God. Maybe this is a healthy reminder to those who put too much emphasis on the study of Bible prophecy.

A Key Moment in Second Thessalonians:

- The day of the Lord *(2 Thessalonians 2)*

FIRST AND SECOND TIMOTHY

These two letters are addressed from Paul to a young church leader named Timothy. The pride Paul feels in his protégé is very clear, but that doesn't stop him from offering a good deal of advice and instruction on how to be a better pastor to his flock. By the time he writes the second letter—probably Paul's last—the relationship seems even closer, and Paul encourages Timothy to *finish the race.*

Some Key Moments in First and Second Timothy:

- Qualifications for church leadership *(1 Timothy 3)*
- Responsibility to those in need *(1 Timothy 5)*
- Remaining faithful *(2 Timothy 3–4)*

TITUS

Like Timothy, Titus is a young church leader whom Paul encourages and instructs. In this letter he writes about very specific guidelines regarding qualifications of church leadership and the conduct of the church. His two key themes are the primacy of moral character and the importance of sound doctrine.

A Key Moment in Titus:

• Pastoral ministry *(Titus 2)*

PHILEMON

Onesimus was a slave in Colossae who escaped from his master, Philemon, and made his way to Rome. There in Rome he became a Christian through the ministry of Paul. Interestingly, Philemon had been tutored in faith by Paul some years earlier. So Paul writes a short personal letter to Philemon asking him to forgive

Onesimus and accept him back as a brother in Christ.

~

HEBREWS

So…how does Christianity fit into the rich heritage of Judaism? That's the topic of this letter to Hebrew Christians. Its author (probably not Paul because the style of this letter is very different from Paul's letters) argues that Christianity is the fulfillment of Judaism. Reviewing Old Testament history, the author demonstrates that everything in the tradition—priesthood, sacrifices, covenant, the Law—points toward rich fulfillment in Jesus Christ and His work as the superior Priest and Prophet.

Some Key Moments in Hebrews:

- The superiority of Christ's priesthood *(Hebrews 5–8)*

- The faith "hall of fame" *(Hebrews 11)*

JAMES

If salvation comes through grace and faith, then where do good works fit in? That is the question posed and answered in this letter by James the brother of Jesus. Because he believes that good works are the natural outgrowth of an authentic faith, this letter is filled with practical advice about how to put faith into action. James helps believers think about how their faith is related to the way they talk, the way they spend their money, and the way they relate to the world around them.

Some Key Moments in James:

- The proper attitude toward money *(James 2)*
- Taming the tongue *(James 3)*

FIRST AND SECOND PETER

Suffering is a universal part of the human experience. And it was a very immediate reality to the early Christians, who were often severely persecuted for their faith. The author of these two letters, the apostle Peter, certainly knew suffering firsthand and eventually gave his life for the cause of the Gospel. In the first letter, he encourages Christians to hang onto their faith, despite the difficulties, and promises that suffering is a prelude to glory. In the second letter, Peter points toward the hope Christians can have because Jesus is coming again.

Some Key Moments in First and Second Peter:

- The purpose of suffering *(1 Peter 2–4)*
- The danger of false teaching *(2 Peter 2)*

FIRST, SECOND, AND THIRD JOHN

These three letters from the apostle John are written to counter a major threat to early Christianity—the teachings of the Gnostics, a sect that challenged the orthodox view of who Jesus was and how Christians should live out their faith in Him. The Gnostics' view of sin was such that the actions of the body really didn't matter. John argues that a pure life is of utmost importance and that love is the primary sign of a vibrant faith.

A Key Moment from First, Second, and Third John

- Righteous living and brotherly love
  (1 John 3–4)

~

JUDE

Jude, written by a brother of James and Jesus, is another letter emphasizing the importance of correct doctrine. He challenges the false teachings that were making their way into the church. Jude also calls believers to live in the holiness that finds its foundation in a true faith.

~

REVELATION

Some Christians spend more time studying Revelation than just about any other book of the Bible. Others neglect it almost entirely, considering it puzzling and confusing. There is no question that it contains some of the most difficult and obscure passages in all of Scripture. Therefore, it should come as no surprise that Christians continue to argue about its correct interpretation.

Some see it as a prophecy of the future events of the last days. Others see it as a symbolic picture of the church in an age of intense suffering. Perhaps we can all agree on this much: In one sense it is the fifth Gospel, John's portrayal of the risen Jesus (the Lamb) who will eventually conquer all the powers of evil that oppose God's kingdom. That is a message of much comfort to both the original readers of the book and Christians today. In the book of Revelation, we see how the story will end—with the triumph of God over all manner of evil and the creation of a new heaven and a new earth.

Some Key Moments in Revelation:

- Letters to the seven churches *(Revelation 2–3)*
- The vision of the Lamb *(Revelation 4–5)*
- Seven seals, seven trumpets, seven bowls *(Revelation 6–16)*
- New heaven and new earth *(Revelation 20–22)*

Part Three

The Greatest Book in the World

GREAT MOMENTS IN THE HISTORY OF THE BIBLE

c. 400 BC	Malachi, the last book of the Old Testament, is written.
c. 300 BC	The Septuagint, the translation of the Old Testament from Hebrew into Greek, is complete.
90 AD	The Council of Jamnia establishes the Jewish canon of the Old Testament.
367 AD	Athanasius lists the approved books of the New Testament.
382 AD	Jerome translates the Bible into Latin (the Vulgate).
397 AD	The Third Council of Carthage approves the New Testament canon (as we have it now).
800 AD	The Book of Kells is produced by Irish monks.
1205 AD	Chapters and verses are added to the books of the Bible.
1380 AD	John Wycliffe translates the Bible into English.
1456 AD	Johannes Gutenberg prints the Bible with his new invention, the printing press.
1534 AD	Martin Luther translates the Bible into the common language of German.
1560 AD	The Geneva Bible is printed.

| 1611 AD | The Authorized Bible, or the King James Version, is produced. |
| 1947 AD | Numerous biblical books are discovered among Dead Sea Scrolls. |

TEN OF THE MOST POPULAR BIBLE TRANSLATIONS

1. *The Authorized* or *King James Version* (1611) is a beautiful and lyrical translation that has had an incalculable effect on the English language. Today some complain that the grandiose and somewhat outdated language makes it difficult to understand.

2. *The Revised Standard Version* (1952) is a somewhat more modern translation that attempted to be very accurate, though some feel it is influenced by liberal theological perspectives—it was updated in 1989 as the *New Revised Standard Version*.

3. *The Jerusalem Bible* (1966) is a modern Catholic translation. One of those who worked on the English translation was J.R.R. Tolkien. Its notes and introductions reflect a more liberal theological bent.

4. *The New American Bible* (1970) is the official English translation of the Catholic church.

5. *The New American Standard Bible* (1971) is a very literal word-for-word translation influenced by conservative theology. It is accurate, but sometimes awkward in its sentence constructions and lacking in literary grace.

6. *The Living Bible* (1971) is a paraphrase by Kenneth Taylor, who wanted to translate the Bible into conversational English for the sake of his children. It became a bestseller and made the Bible very accessible, but it takes some translation liberties along the way. It was updated in 1996 as the *New Living Bible* and its accuracy was much improved.

7. *The New International Version* (1978) has become the Bible of choice for many conservative Christians and is the current bestselling translation. It is a translation based upon thought-by-thought, rather than word-by-word, principles of translation. It was updated and made more gender-neutral in 2005 as *Today's New International Version.*

8. *The New King James Version* (1982) is a thorough updating of the *King James Version* with the attempt to retain some of the familiar and beautiful phrasing.

9. *The English Standard Version* (2001) is another translation based upon conservative theological principles.

10. *The Message* (2002) is a very free and colloquial paraphrase by Eugene Peterson that takes some interpretive liberties, but it is very readable and sometimes quite striking in its phrasing.

TWELVE MEMORABLE THINGS PEOPLE SAID ABOUT THE BIBLE

1. *The studious perusal of the Sacred Volume will make better citizens, better fathers, and better husbands.* (Thomas Jefferson)

2. *This Great Book is the best gift God has given to man.* (Abraham Lincoln)

3. *I know the Bible is inspired because it inspires me.* (D.L. Moody)

4. *The Bible is a book that has been read more and examined less than any book that ever existed.* (Thomas Paine)

5. *Whatever merit there is in anything that I have written is simply due to the fact that when I was a child my mother daily read me a part of the Bible and daily made me learn a part of it by heart.* (John Ruskin)

6. *The Bible is no mere book, but a Living Creature, with a power that conquers all that oppose it.* (Napoleon Bonaparte)

7. *In all my perplexities and distresses, the Bible has never failed to give me light and strength.* (Robert E. Lee)

8. *Bible reading is an education in itself.* (Alfred Lord Tennyson)

9. *The New Testament is the very best book that ever was or ever will be known in the world.* (Charles Dickens)

10. *The existence of the Bible, as a book for the people, is the greatest benefit which the human race has ever experienced. Every attempt to belittle it is a crime against humanity.* (Immanuel Kant)

11. *To the influence of this Book we are indebted for all the progress made in true civilization, and to this we must look as our guide in the future.* (Ulysses S. Grant)

12. *There is a Book worth all other books which were ever printed.* (Patrick Henry)

FIVE THINGS THE BIBLE SAYS ABOUT THE BIBLE

1. *Your word is a lamp to my feet and a light for my path.* (Psalm 119:105)

2. *The grass withers and the flowers fall, but the word of our God stands forever.* (Isaiah 40:8)

3. *Jesus answered, "It is written: 'Man does not live on bread alone, but on every word that comes from the mouth of God.'"* (Matthew 4:4)

4. *All Scripture is God-breathed and is useful for teaching, rebuking, correcting and training in righteousness, so that the man of God may be thoroughly equipped for every good work.* (2 Timothy 3:16)

5. *Above all, you must understand that no prophecy of Scripture came about by the prophet's own interpretation. For the prophecy never had its origin in the will of man, but men spoke from God as they were carried along by the Holy Spirit.* (2 Peter 1:20-21)

FOURTEEN FAMILIAR PHRASES THAT ORIGINATED IN THE BIBLE

1. *The blind leading the blind* (Matthew 15:14)

2. *Scapegoat* (Leviticus 16:10)

3. *By the skin of your teeth* (Job 19:20)

4. *Fat of the land* (Genesis 45:18)

5. *Drop in the bucket* (Isaiah 40:15)

6. *Sour grapes* (Ezekiel 18:2)

7. *Going the extra mile* (Matthew 5:41)

8. *Turn the other cheek* (Matthew 5:39)

9. *It's better to give than to receive* (Acts 20:35)

10. *Set your teeth on edge* (Jeremiah 31:29)

11. *Put words in his mouth* (Exodus 4:15;
    Deuteronomy 18:18; 2 Samuel 14:3; Jeremiah 1:9)

12. *A fly in the ointment* (Ecclesiastes 10:1)

13. *Out of the mouths of babes* (Psalm 8:2)

14. *A lamb to the slaughter* (Isaiah 53:7)

FIFTEEN FAMOUS PAINTERS WHO CREATED ART BASED ON THE BIBLE

1. **Giotto** (1267–1337). The first genius of art in the Italian Renaissance, he painted huge frescoes at the Arena Chapel in Padua, including *The Adoration of the Magi* and *The Mourning of Christ.*

2. **Bosch** (1450–1516). In addition to some rather harrowing depictions of hell, Bosch painted *Christ Mocked* and *Christ Carrying the Cross.*

3. **Leonardo da Vinci** (1452–1519). *The Last Supper* and *Adoration of the Magi* are among his masterpieces.

4. **Dürer** (1471–1528). *The Four Horsemen of the Apocalypse* is part of a series of woodcuts inspired by the book of Revelation. A very committed Christian, he also painted Adam and Eve and other biblical subjects.

5. **Michelangelo** (1475–1564). He created the

famous statues *David* and *Moses*. The huge painting *The Last Judgment* and, of course, the paintings on the ceiling of the Sistine Chapel are also Michelangelo's masterpieces.

6. **Raphael** (1483–1520). He painted many works with biblical themes, including *The Deposition*.

7. **Titian** (1490–1576). *St. John on Patmos* and *Crowning With Thorns* are among his masterpieces.

8. **Pieter Brueghel** (1525–1569). *The Tower of Babel* and *Massacre of the Innocents* were painted by Brueghel.

9. **Caravaggio** (1573–1610). He painted many biblical subjects including *Conversion of St. Paul*, *The Calling of Matthew*, and *The Supper at Emmaus*.

10. **Poussin** (1594–1665). *Moses Striking the Rock* is one of his most famous paintings.

11. **Rembrandt** (1606–1669). He is one of

the most prolific painters of biblical topics. Among his many etchings and paintings are such powerful works as *The Return of the Prodigal Son, The Raising of the Cross,* and *Belshazzar's Feast.*

12. **Dante Rossetti** (1828–1882). This famous painter created a wonderful painting of Gabriel's visit to Mary, *The Annunciation.*

13. **Georges Rouault** (1871–1958). One of the great modern painters and a believer, his works include *Christ and the High Priest* and *Christ Mocked by Soldiers.*

14. **Marc Chagall** (1887–1985). There is an entire museum in Nice, France, dedicated to the biblical art of this modern Jewish painter.

15. **Salvador Dali** (1904–1989). He painted a mystical version of the *Sacrament of the Last Supper.*

TWELVE MORE MEMORABLE THINGS PEOPLE HAVE SAID ABOUT THE BIBLE

1. *Western civilization is founded upon the Bible; all our ideas, our wisdom, our philosophy, our literature, our art, our ideals come more from the Bible than all other books put together.* (William Lyon Phelps)

2. *After more than 60 years of almost daily reading of the Bible, I never fail to find it always new and marvelously in tune with the changing needs of every day.* (Cecil B. DeMille)

3. *The Bible grows more beautiful as we grow in our understanding of it.* (Johann Wolfgang von Goethe)

4. *I account the Scriptures of God the most sublime philosophy.* (Isaac Newton)

5. *The one use of the Bible is to make us look at Jesus, that through Him we might know His*

Father and our Father, His God and our God.
(George MacDonald)

6. *The whole counsel of God, concerning all things necessary for His own glory, man's salvation, faith, and life, is either expressly set down in Scripture, or by good and necessary consequence may be deduced from Scripture: unto which nothing at any time is to be added, whether by new revelations of the Spirit, or traditions of men.* (Westminster Confession)

7. *The Word of God well understood and religiously obeyed is the shortest route to spiritual perfection. And we must not select a few favorite passages to the exclusion of others. Nothing less than the whole Bible can make a whole Christian.* (A.W. Tozer)

8. *Thus Scripture is a book, to which there belongeth not only reading but also the right Expositor and Revealer, to wit, the Holy Spirit. Where He openeth not Scripture, it is not understood.* (Martin Luther)

9. *The Bible is not merely a record of the revelation; it is part of the revelation. It is not a quarry for the historian, but a fountain for the soul.* (P.T. Forsyth)

10. *Scripture is like a pair of spectacles which dispels the darkness and gives us a clear view of God.* (John Calvin)

11. *The truth of God is the only treasure for which we seek, and the Scripture is the only field in which we dig for it.* (Charles Spurgeon)

12. *When you read God's Word, you must constantly be saying to yourself, "It is talking to me, and about me."* (Soren Kierkegaard)

TEN GREAT PIECES OF CLASSICAL MUSIC BASED ON BIBLICAL TEXTS

1. *St. John's Passion* by Johann Sebastian Bach (1724)

2. *St. Matthew's Passion* by Johann Sebastian Bach (1727)

3. *Messiah* by George Frideric Handel (1742)

4. *The Creation* by Franz Joseph Haydn (1800)

5. *Moses in Egypt* by Gioacchino Rossini (1818)

6. *St. Paul* by Felix Mendelssohn (1836)

7. *Elijah* by Felix Mendelssohn (1846)

8. *Samson and Delilah* by Camille Saint-Saëns (1877)

9. *Symphony of Psalms* by Igor Stravinsky (1930)

10. *Moses and Aaron* by Arnold Schoenberg (1932)

THE OLD TESTAMENT ACCORDING TO FILM

*(Some Movies About
Old Testament Stories)*

Samson and Delilah (1949) is a Cecil B. DeMille blockbuster.

David and Bathsheba (1951) starred Gregory Peck and Susan Hayward.

The Ten Commandments (1956), starring Charlton Heston, is probably the most famous version of the story of the Exodus.

Sodom and Gomorrah (1962) is an Italian and American production starring Stewart Granger.

The Bible (1966) covers many biblical stories of the Old Testament with an all-star cast.

King David (1985) starred Richard Gere as David.

The Prince of Egypt (1998) is an animated film about the life of Moses.

Jonah: A VeggieTales Movie (2002) is a child's favorite—animated vegetables tell the biblical story of Jonah.

One Night With the King (2006) is the story of Esther.

THE NEW TESTAMENT ACCORDING TO FILM

*(Some Movies About
New Testament Stories)*

Ben Hur (1959) is a famous, imaginative spectacle constructed around the events of the Gospels.

The Big Fisherman (1959) is Hollywood's version of the life of Peter.

King of Kings (1961) is a classic version of the life of Christ.

The Gospel According to St. Matthew (1964) is an artistic Marxist interpretation.

The Greatest Story Ever Told (1965) is a star-studded film about the life of Jesus.

Jesus Christ Superstar (1973) is the infamous rock opera about Jesus.

Gospel Road: A Story of Jesus (1973) is Johnny Cash's film tribute to Jesus.

Jesus of Nazareth (1977) is the beautifully-filmed British and Italian production by Franco Zeffirelli.

Jesus (1979) is Campus Crusade's literal version of the Jesus story.

Peter and Paul (1981) is an underappreciated British television miniseries starring Anthony Hopkins as Paul.

The Visual Bible: Matthew (1997) is the word-for-word depiction of Matthew's Gospel.

The Passion of the Christ (2004) is Mel Gibson's vivid depiction, both violent and beautiful.

The Nativity (2006) is a straightforward modern version.

TEN MORE MEMORABLE THINGS PEOPLE HAVE SAID ABOUT THE BIBLE

1. *The Bible is a harp with a thousand strings. Play on one to the exclusion of its relationship to the others, and you will develop discord. Play on all of them, keeping them in their places in the divine scale, and you will hear heavenly music all the time.* (William P. White)

2. *The Word of God hidden in the heart is a stubborn voice to suppress.* (Billy Graham)

3. *The greatest proof that the Bible is inspired is that it has stood so much bad preaching.* (A.T. Robertson)

4. *To preach the Bible as "the handbook for life," or as the answer to every question, rather than the revelation of Christ, is to turn the Bible into an entirely different book. This is how the Pharisees approached Scripture, however, as we can see clearly from the questions they asked Jesus...For the Pharisees, the Scriptures were a*

source of trivia for life's dilemmas.
(Michael Horton)

5. *It is impossible for me to recant unless I am proved to be wrong by the testimony of Scripture. My conscience is bound to the Word of God.* (Martin Luther)

6. *The Bible is not an end in itself, but a means to bring men to an intimate and satisfying knowledge of God, that they may enter into Him, that they may delight in His Presence, may taste and know the inner sweetness of the very God Himself in the core and center of their hearts.* (A.W. Tozer)

7. *The Bible is to me the most precious thing in the world just because it tells me the story of Jesus.* (George MacDonald)

8. *The Bible was never intended to be a book for scholars and specialists only. From the very beginning it was intended to be everybody's book, and that's what it continues to be.* (F.F. Bruce)

9. *We ought to listen to the Scriptures with the greatest caution, for as far as understanding of them goes, we are as but little children.*
   (Augustine)

10. *Nobody ever outgrows Scripture; the Book widens and deepens with our years.*
    (Charles Spurgeon)

Part Four

≈≋≈

Help for Every Day
from God's Word

TEN VERSES FOR WHEN YOU FEEL AFRAID

1. *The LORD is my light and my salvation— whom shall I fear? The LORD is the stronghold of my life—of whom shall I be afraid?* (Psalm 27:1)

2. *In God I trust; I will not be afraid.* (Psalm 56:11)

3. *He will cover you with his feathers, and under his wings you will find refuge; his faithfulness will be your shield and rampart. You will not fear the terror of night, nor the arrow that flies by day, nor the pestilence that stalks in the darkness, nor the plague that destroys at midday.* (Psalm 91:4-6)

4. *Have no fear of sudden disaster or of the ruin that overtakes the wicked, for the LORD will be your confidence and will keep your foot from being snared.* (Proverbs 3:25-26)

5. *Fear of man will prove to be a snare, but*

whoever trusts in the LORD is kept safe.
(Proverbs 29:25)

6. *Peace I leave with you; my peace I give you. I do not give to you as the world gives. Do not let your hearts be troubled and do not be afraid.* (John 14:27)

7. *I have told you these things, so that in me you may have peace. In this world you will have trouble. But take heart! I have overcome the world.* (John 16:33)

8. *And we know that in all things God works for the good of those who love him, who have been called according to his purpose.* (Romans 8:28)

9. *We say with confidence, "The Lord is my helper; I will not be afraid. What can man do to me?"* (Hebrews 13:6)

10. *But perfect love drives out fear.* (1 John 4:18)

ELEVEN VERSES FOR WHEN YOU NEED COMFORT

1. *The LORD is a refuge for the oppressed, a stronghold in times of trouble.* (Psalm 9:9)

2. *The LORD is my rock, my fortress and my deliverer; my God is my rock, in whom I take refuge. He is my shield and the horn of my salvation, my stronghold.* (Psalm 18:2)

3. *The LORD is my shepherd, I shall not be in want...* (Psalm 23:1) (Read the entire psalm!)

4. *Weeping may remain for a night, but rejoicing comes in the morning.* (Psalm 30:5)

5. *The LORD is close to the brokenhearted and saves those who are crushed in spirit.* (Psalm 34:18)

6. *God is our refuge and strength, an ever-present help in trouble. Therefore we will not fear, though the earth give way and the mountains fall into the heart of the sea.* (Psalm 46:1-2)

7. *Though you have made me see troubles, many*

and bitter, you will restore my life again; from the depths of the earth you will again bring me up. You will increase my honor and comfort me once again. (Psalm 71:20-21)

8. *The LORD is good, a refuge in times of trouble. He cares for those who trust in him.* (Nahum 1:7)

9. *Come to me, all you who are weary and burdened, and I will give you rest.* (Matthew 11:28)

10. *Peace I leave with you; my peace I give you. I do not give to you as the world gives. Do not let your hearts be troubled and do not be afraid.* (John 14:27)

11. *Praise be to the God and Father of our Lord Jesus Christ, the Father of all compassion and the God of all comfort, who comforts us in all our troubles, so that we can comfort those in any trouble with the comfort we ourselves have received from God.* (2 Corinthians 1:3-4)

TEN VERSES FOR WHEN YOU FEEL DEPRESSED

1. *Why are you downcast, O my soul? Why so disturbed within me? Put your hope in God, for I will yet praise him, my Savior and my God.* (Psalm 43:5)

2. *Call upon me in the day of trouble; I will deliver you, and you will honor me.* (Psalm 50:15)

3. *Cast your cares upon the LORD and he will sustain you.* (Psalm 55:22)

4. *I wait for the LORD, my soul waits, and in his word I put my hope.* (Psalm 130:5)

5. *He heals the brokenhearted and binds up their wounds.* (Psalm 147:3)

6. *Those who hope in the LORD will renew their strength. They will soar on wings like eagles; they will run and not grow weary, they will walk and not be faint.* (Isaiah 40:31)

7. *Do not fear, for I am with you; do not be*

*dismayed, for I am your God. I will strengthen
you and help you; I will uphold you with my
righteous right hand.* (Isaiah 41:10)

8. *I called on your name, O LORD, from the
depths of the pit. You heard my plea: Do not
close your ears to my cry for relief. You came
near when I called you, and you said, "Do not
fear."* (Lamentations 3:55-57)

9. *Come to me, all you who are weary and
burdened, and I will give you rest.* (Matthew
11:28)

10. *Now to him who is able to do immeasurably
more than all we ask or imagine, according
to his power that is at work within us, to him
be glory in the church and in Christ Jesus
throughout all generations, for ever and ever!
Amen.* (Ephesians 3:20-21)

≈

TEN VERSES FOR WHEN YOU FEEL GUILTY

1. *Blessed is he whose transgressions are forgiven, whose sins are covered. Blessed is the man whose sin the LORD does not count against him and in whose spirit there is no deceit… Then I acknowledged my sin to you and did not cover up my iniquity. I said, "I will confess my transgressions to the LORD"—and you forgave the guilt of my sin.* (Psalm 32:1-2,5)

2. *As far as the east is from the west, so far has he removed our transgressions from us.* (Psalm 103:12)

3. *If you, O LORD, kept a record of sins, O LORD, who could stand? But with you there is forgiveness; therefore you are feared.* (Psalm 130:3-4)

4. *I, even I, am he who blots out your transgressions, for my own sake, and remembers your sins no more.* (Isaiah 43:25)

5. *There is now no condemnation for those who are in Christ Jesus.* (Romans 8:1)

6. *If anyone is in Christ, he is a new creation; the old has gone, the new has come!* (2 Corinthians 5:17)

7. *In him we have redemption through his blood, the forgiveness of sins, in accordance with the riches of God's grace that he lavished upon us with all wisdom and understanding.* (Ephesians 1:7-8)

8. *He forgave us all our sins, having canceled the written code, with its regulations, that was against us and that stood opposed to us; he took it away, nailing it to the cross.* (Colossians 2:13-14)

9. *I will forgive their wickedness and will remember their sins no more.* (Hebrews 8:12)

10. *If we confess our sins, he is faithful and just and will forgive us our sins and purify us from all unrighteousness.* (1 John 1:9)

FIVE VERSES FOR WHEN
YOU FEEL LONELY

1. *By day the LORD directs his love, at night his song is with me—a prayer to the God of my life.* (Psalm 42:8)

2. *He heals the brokenhearted and binds up their wounds.* (Psalm 147:3)

3. *Can a mother forget the baby at her breast and have no compassion on the child she has borne? Though she may forget, I will not forget you! See, I have engraved you on the palms of my hands.* (Isaiah 49:15-16)

4. *Surely I am with you always, to the very end of the age.* (Matthew 28:20)

5. *I am convinced that neither death nor life, neither angels nor demons, neither the present nor the future, nor any powers, neither height nor depth, nor anything else in all creation, will be able to separate us from the love of God that is in Christ Jesus our Lord.* (Romans 8:38-39)

SEVEN VERSES FOR WHEN YOU FEEL STRESSED AND WORRIED

1. *Cast your cares on the LORD and he will sustain you; he will never let the righteous fall.* (Psalm 55:22)

2. *You will keep in perfect peace him whose mind is steadfast, because he trusts in you. Trust in the LORD forever, for the LORD, the LORD, is the Rock eternal.* (Isaiah 26:3-4)

3. *Come to me, all you who are weary and burdened, and I will give you rest.* (Matthew 11:28)

4. *Peace I leave with you; my peace I give you. I do not give to you as the world gives. Do not let your hearts be troubled and do not be afraid.* (John 14:27)

5. *We know that in all things God works for the good of those who love him, who have been called according to his purpose.* (Romans 8:28)

6. *Do not be anxious about anything, but in everything, by prayer and petition, with thanksgiving, present your requests to God. And the peace of God, which transcends all understanding, will guard your hearts and your minds in Christ Jesus.* (Philippians 4:6-7)

7. *My God will meet all your needs according to his glorious riches in Christ Jesus.* (Philippians 4:19)

EIGHT VERSES FOR WHEN YOU ARE TEMPTED

1. *May the words of my mouth and the meditation of my heart be pleasing in your sight, O LORD, my Rock and my Redeemer.* (Psalm 19:14)

2. *Set a guard over my mouth, O LORD; keep watch over the door of my lips. Let not my heart be drawn to what is evil, to take part in wicked deeds with men who are evildoers.* (Psalm 141:3-4)

3. *Because he himself suffered when he was tempted, he is able to help those who are being tempted.* (Hebrews 2:18)

4. *In all these things we are more than conquerors through him who loved us.* (Romans 8:37)

5. *No temptation has seized you except what is common to man. And God is faithful; he will not let you be tempted beyond what you can bear. But when you are tempted, he will also*

provide a way out so that you can stand up under it. (1 Corinthians 10:13)

6. *We do not have a high priest who is unable to sympathize with our weaknesses, but we have one who has been tempted in every way, just as we are—yet was without sin. Let us then approach the throne of grace with confidence, so that we may receive mercy and find grace to help us in our time of need.* (Hebrews 4:15-16)

7. *When tempted, no one should say, "God is tempting me." For God cannot be tempted by evil, nor does he tempt anyone; but each one is tempted when, by his own evil desire, he is dragged away and enticed.* (James 1:13-14)

8. *The Lord knows how to rescue godly men from trials.* (2 Peter 2:9)

LETTING GOD'S WORD
CHANGE YOUR LIFE

Make Bible reading a habit.
Try to read a little every day.

~

Don't settle for a simplistic understanding.
Study and learn and grow.

~

Reading the Bible is a life-long pursuit.
Read it all. Read it again!

~

Pray passages of the Bible into your life. Read
with God at your side and prayer on your lips.

~

Study with friends. They'll see things
that you might have missed.

~

Let the Bible do its work on you;
transforming your mind, your heart,
your emotions, and your spirit.

***Other Great Harvest House Books
to Help You Learn About the Bible***

Knowing the Bible 101
Bruce Bickel & Stan Jantz

The Bare Bones Bible™ Handbook
Jim George

How to Study the Bible for Yourself
Tim LaHaye

The Quick-Start Beginner's Guide to the Bible
J. Stephen Lang

Knowing and Loving the Bible
Catherine Martin

What Does the Bible Say About…?
Ron Rhodes